ic
12.20.10

Fossils

by Melissa Stewart

Heinemann Library
CHICAGO, ILLINOIS

Designed by Ox and Company

An Editorial Directions book

Printed in China

06 05 04 03
10 9 8 7 6 5 4 3 2

Library of Congress Cataloging-in-Publication Data
Stewart, Melissa.
  Fossils / Melissa Stewart.
     p. cm.—(Rocks and minerals)
Includes bibliographical references and index.
Summary: Provides an overview of fossils including how they were formed, what
they are made of, their historical implications, how they are dated, and how to
hunt for them.
  ISBN: 1-58810-255-6 (HC), 1-4034-0091-1 (Pbk.)
  1. Fossils—Juvenile literature. [1. Fossils. 2. Paleontology.] I. Title.
  QE714.5 .S74 2002
  560—dc21   2001002756

Acknowledgments
The author and publishers are grateful to the following for permission to reproduce copyright material:

Photographs ©: Cover background, A.J. Copley/Visuals Unlimited, Inc.; cover foreground, Lester V. Bergman/Corbis; p. 4,
James P. Rowan; p. 5, Scott Berner/Visuals Unlimited, Inc.; p. 7, Jack K. Clark/The Image Works; p. 8, Dick Keen/Visuals
Unlimited, Inc.; p. 9, James P. Rowan; p. 10, Ken Lucas/Visuals Unlimited, Inc.; pp. 11, 12, A.J. Copley/Visuals Unlimited,
Inc.; p. 13, Tom & Therisa Stack/Tom Stack & Associates; p. 16, A.J. Copley/Visuals Unlimited, Inc.; p. 18, Tom
Smart/Gamma Liaison/Hulton Archive; p. 20, James P. Rowan; p. 21, Mark Wilson/Newsmakers/Gamma Liaison/Hulton
Archive; p. 22, A.J. Copley/Visuals Unlimited, Inc.; p. 23, Reuters New Media, Inc./Corbis; p. 24, Tom Bean; p. 25, Joe
McDonald/Tom Stack & Associates; p. 26, John D. Cunningham/Visuals Unlimited, Inc.; p. 27, Rob & Ann
Simpson/Simpson's Nature Photography; p. 28, Patrick Aventurier/Gamma Liaison/Hulton Archive; p. 29, Ken Lucas/Visuals
Unlimited, Inc.

Every effort has been made to contact copyright holders of any material reproduced in this book. Any omissions will be rectified
in subsequent printings if notice is given to the publisher.

Some words are shown in bold, **like this.** You can find out what they mean by looking in the glossary.

Contents

What Are Fossils?

You've probably seen fossils in a museum or on television, but did you know that you might be able to find some fossils closer to home? You might even find some in your own backyard or at a local park. You probably won't uncover the bones of a ferocious dinosaur or a giant mammoth, but fossils of small sea animals can be found just about anywhere on Earth. Fossils are more common than you might think.

This ancient trilobite fossil is on display at the Houston Museum of Natural Science in Texas. Trilobites are **extinct** sea animals that lived on Earth between 570 and 250 million years ago.

There are many kinds of fossils. Some fossils are the remains of plants, animals, and other creatures that were once alive. Examples include giant dinosaur bones, sharks' teeth, all kinds of seashells, and imprints of leaves or other plant parts. These fossils show us what ancient life forms looked like even though they have been dead for millions of years.

DID YOU KNOW?

The word *fossil* comes from a Latin word meaning "something dug out of the ground." Fossils are often dug out of the ground, but not everything we dig up is a fossil.

Other fossils tell us something about how ancient creatures lived. For example, a trail of dinosaur footprints in hard rock is a kind of fossil. The footprints can help scientists figure out how big the dinosaur was and how fast it moved. By studying the fossils of eggs and nests, scientists can learn important information about ancient animal families. Fossils of tooth marks provide clues about where prehistoric predators lived and how they hunted.

Fossils can teach scientists a great deal about creatures that lived long ago. They also help us understand how life has **evolved** and how Earth has changed over time. Fossils can even help scientists learn about the environment on Earth millions of years ago. For instance, if the fossil of a sea creature is found away from a coast, a scientist knows that that land used to be under water.

Scientists can learn a lot by studying dinosaur footprints. Tracks like these in Texas tell researchers that several different kinds of dinosaurs once roamed this region.

FOSSIL OR FAKE?

Sometimes rock formations can fool fossil hunters. Round clumps of soft, white chalk and black, flaky flint may look like parts of plants or animals. But a closer look can reveal the truth. These fake fossils do not have as much detail as real fossils.

How Fossils Form

Plants and animals die all the time, but most do not become fossils. Sometimes they are eaten by animals. Sometimes they rot. Only a very small number of living things become fossils.

Fossils are rare because conditions must be just right for them to form. A life form must be buried quickly in a place where there is very little air. That's why 90 percent of all fossils are found in ground that was once at the bottom of an ocean or a large lake.

A.

B.

When a fish dies, it sinks to the muddy seafloor. The soft body parts of the fish slowly rot until only the hard bones are left.

As more time passes, minerals dissolved in the water seep into the bones and gradually replace them. Eventually, the minerals harden and form stone.

The mold (left) of a trilobite is the impression left in the rock after an animal's body has decayed. When a trilobite's shell is replaced with new minerals, a cast (right) forms.

C.

In the meantime, layers of mud, sand, and other **sediments** pile up on top of the fish. As the weight of all these layers presses down, the sediments harden and stick together to form **sedimentary rock.**

Sometimes all the remains of a creature are dissolved away. But because layers of mud hardened around it, an imprint of the creature is left behind in the rock. This kind of fossil is called a **mold.** A **cast** of the creature may also form if the mold fills with **minerals** that harden and become solid stone.

Bones, Teeth, and Shells

Most fossils form from the hard parts of creatures' bodies. Some of the most common fossils show us the razor-sharp teeth of **extinct** sharks and the spiraling shells of ancient sea creatures, such as ammonites and nautiloids. Although many of these creatures no longer exist, corals, sea stars, clams, and scallops are still common today.

Some of the most exciting fossils show us the giant bones of ferocious, meat-eating dinosaurs, such as *Tyrannosaurus*, and large, clumsy plant-eaters, such as *Diplodocus*. By carefully piecing fossil bones together, scientists can often build part—or even all—of an animal's **skeleton.** Once

DID YOU KNOW?

By studying fossils of sharks' teeth (right), scientists have discovered that some ancient sharks may have been twice as big as today's sharks.

scientists know an animal's size and shape, they can often figure out how it lived and what it ate.

Most of these fossils form between layers of **sedimentary rocks,** such as limestone, sandstone, or shale. They may also be preserved in peat, tar, or ice.

TERRIFYING TAR

Los Angeles, California, is one of the busiest cities in the world today. But forty thousand years ago, the area was covered with moist grasslands. Mammoths, early horses, giant ground sloths, and saber-tooth cats lived there. How do scientists know this? They have found fossils of these animals in the Rancho La Brea Tar Pits—large, shallow puddles of ancient asphalt. You can still visit these tar pits today, and see replicas of ancient creatures (above)!

When it rained, water pooled on top of the sticky, black asphalt. Thirsty animals sometimes tried to drink the water—and thus became trapped in the tar. When a predator passed by, it saw the helpless animals. Thinking it had found an easy meal, the predator jumped into the tar. Then it got stuck too. By studying fossils from the tar pits, scientists have learned a lot about the animals that lived in southern California 40,000 years ago.

Some Common Fossils

Because fossils are most likely to form in underwater environments, it is not surprising that the most common fossils are the remains of ocean creatures.

Ammonites are **extinct** now, but their close relative—the nautilus—is still around. Ammonites had spiral-shaped shells with chambers. Some people think an ammonite shell looks like a ram's horn.

Trilobites are also extinct, but some of their distant relatives—lobsters, spiders, and insects—still live on Earth. These small sea creatures first appeared on Earth about 540 million years ago and were very common all over the world for about 300 million years. At their height, there were more

These ammonite fossils were found in England. Ammonites first appeared on Earth more than 400 million years ago. Their fossils are often found in layers of limestone.

than 10,000 different kinds of trilobites.

Each trilobite had an oval body and a hard, tough outer layer that acted like a **skeleton.** It could walk on the seafloor or swim in shallow water. When a trilobite felt threatened, it curled up in a tight ball until the danger passed. Scientists have found some trilobite fossils in that rolled-up position.

Sea stars, brittle stars, sea urchins, and sea snails all appeared on Earth about 450 million years ago. Unlike trilobites and ammonites, they are still alive today. In the past, these animals lived in warm, shallow seas. Today they can be found along seashores all over the world.

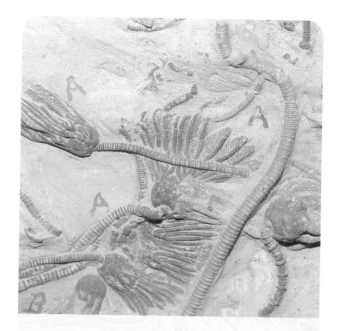

PLANT OR ANIMAL?

If you've ever seen a living sea lily or the fossil of an ancient one, you probably thought you were looking at a plant. But sea lilies aren't plants—they are animals. They are closely related to sea stars and sea urchins. In some parts of North America, sea lily fossils are easy to find.

Fish were the first animals with a backbone and a skeleton inside their bodies. They appeared on Earth about 440 million years ago. Early fish had heavy armor. The easiest fish fossils to find are sharks' teeth. Once you learn how to spot them, you can find them almost anywhere in the world.

Traces of the Past

Scientists study coprolites of animals (above) to learn about their diets. They also study coprolites of our human ancestors.

Not all fossils are the remains of creatures that lived long ago. **Trace fossils** include animal footprints and trails, tooth marks, coprolites, eggs, and ancient animal homes. These fossils can help scientists understand how, when, and where ancient creatures lived.

Footprints and trails can provide scientists with clues about how an animal moved, how tall it was, and how much it weighed. For example, researchers believe that a grouping of mammoth footprints found in Murray Springs, Arizona, may represent an animal's final steps. At the end of the trail, scientists uncovered the **skeleton** of a

DID YOU KNOW?

In Canada in 1995, fossil hunter Wendy Sloboda found a coprolite the size of two loaves of bread laid end-to-end. It's the biggest sample of dinosaur droppings ever found. The prehistoric poop contained pieces of bone and may have been produced by the king of dinosaurs— *Tyrannosaurus rex.*

Columbian mammoth. Another group of researchers working in Queensland, Australia, found fossil footprints of more than 100 stampeding dinosaurs. They were being chased by a fierce, meat-eating dinosaur.

Coprolites are fossils of animal droppings. They can tell scientists when and where an animal lived and what it ate. Scientists use this information to understand ancient food chains.

Fossils of ancient eggs have been discovered at more than 150 sites in Africa, Asia, Europe, North America, and South America. In some cases, the eggs were still inside the nests where they were laid millions of years ago. The eggs have helped scientists discover how many young these ancient reptiles and birds had at one time, and how much care the parents gave their young. Using an assortment of tiny chisels, acid baths, or high-tech scanning methods, some scientists have been able to take a peek at the tiny animals that were developing inside the eggs.

These ancient dinosaur eggs will never hatch. By studying the eggs, scientists can learn more about the creatures that laid them.

Land on the Move

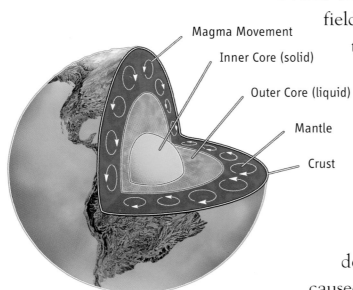

Magma Movement

Inner Core (solid)

Outer Core (liquid)

Mantle

Crust

Fossils can be found anywhere—in fields or deserts, on mountain-tops, or even in blasted rock along the side of the road. At one time, many of these places were underwater. So why are they on solid ground today? Over millions of years, forces deep inside Earth have caused the land to move.

The thin outer layer of Earth is the crust. The next layer, the mantle, is made of magma that is constantly moving. The core is made of an outer liquid core and an inner solid core.

Earth has three layers—the **crust,** the **mantle,** and the **core.** Earth's central core is much hotter than the crust we walk on. As heat from the core moves into the mantle, it cooks the rock to form a thick liquid material called **magma.** Magma can flow, but it flows very slowly. As the hottest magma near the core moves toward the surface, cooler magma moves down to take its place. Over millions of years, magma circles slowly through the mantle.

Earth's crust is broken into pieces that fit together like the pieces of a puzzle. These pieces, called **plates,** float on top of the mantle like rafts on a sea of moving magma. As the magma churns, the plates—and the land on top of them—travel slowly across Earth's surface.

In some parts of the world, plates move apart and create gaps called **rifts.** Magma slowly flows out of the mantle through these rifts and then cools and hardens to form new land or seafloor. Each year, North America and Europe move farther apart because two plates are separating under the Atlantic Ocean.

In other parts of the world, plates crash into one another. Sometimes one plate slides over the other. Then the bottom plate moves down into the mantle where it melts. When two plates hit head-on and push against each other with great force, the land buckles and tall mountains form. The Himalaya Mountains grow taller each year as the Indian-Australian Plate crashes into the Asian Plate. When two plates scrape against each other, the result is a **transform fault,** such as the San Andreas Fault in California and the Dalkey Fault in Ireland. When enough pressure builds up along such a fault, an earthquake occurs.

Mountains may form when two plates hit head-on. The seafloor expands as magma rises through a rift. When one plate moves below another, magma may rise to the surface and escape through a volcano.

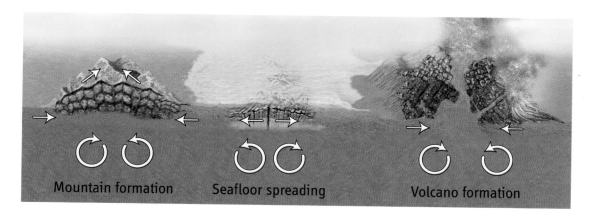

Mountain formation   Seafloor spreading   Volcano formation

How Earth Has Changed

DID YOU KNOW?

The word *Pangaea* means "all lands" in Greek.

Scientists believe Earth formed about 4.6 billion years ago, but it has looked the way it does today for only about 65 million years. Before that, the continents were in different places. As Earth's **plates** have moved, so has the land. New oceans have formed, and old ones have disappeared.

Scientists are still trying to figure out all the ways Earth has changed over time. They think that about 250 million years ago, all of Earth's land formed a giant continent called Pangaea.

Adult mesosaurs were slim and grew to be about 2 feet (0.6 meters) long. They lived in freshwater lakes and ponds.

As time passed, the plates below Pangaea moved apart, and the land broke into two

continents called Laurasia and Gondwanaland. As more time passed, the plates continued to travel across Earth's surface to form the continents we know today. The continents are still on the move. Perhaps, one day, all of Earth's land will come together again and form a third giant continent.

How do scientists know where landmasses were millions of years ago? Many of the most important clues have come from fossils.

By the time Pangaea formed, the ocean was full of fish, and dinosaurs were roaming the land. Scientists have found fossils of the freshwater reptile *Mesosaurus* at the southern tip of Africa and in South America. It is very unlikely that the exact same animal could develop in two different places, and *Mesosaurus* could not swim all the way across the Atlantic Ocean, so scientists know that the two continents were once joined. If you look at the outlines of these continents, you can see how they fit together.

250 million years ago

240 million years ago

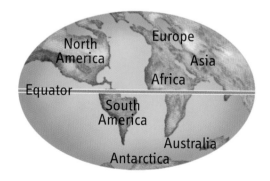

The continents today

Throughout Earth's history, the continents have moved continuously across our planet's surface.

How Old Is That Fossil?

These scientists determined the relative age of their fossil find by studying the surrounding rock. To find the absolute age of the raptor fossil they are digging up, they will need to take samples back to the lab.

You know how old you are because your parents tell you. You can figure out how old a tree is by counting the rings in its trunk. But it's not so easy to find out how old a fossil is.

Scientists can determine a fossil's **relative age** by looking for clues nearby. For example, scientists know that some creatures lived on Earth for only a short time and that others changed dramatically over a short period of time. When they see fossils of these creatures in a rock, they can make a good guess about the age of other fossils nearby.

Scientists can determine a fossil's **absolute age** by performing a variety of tests on the rock it was found in. This kind of testing must be done in a scientific laboratory, so the fossil and some of the surrounding rock must be dug up and removed from the site.

Because scientists want to know what Earth was like when these ancient creatures they find were alive, they have created a **geologic time scale.** This scale divides the last 600 million years—the time during which animals have lived on Earth—into smaller units. During each time period, conditions on Earth were different, so different animals thrived.

GEOLOGIC TIME SCALE

TIME (in millions of years ago)	ERA	PERIOD	DOMINANT ANIMAL LIFE
1.8 to present	Cenozoic	Quaternary	Mammals
65 to 1.8		Tertiary	
146 to 65	Mesozoic	Cretaceous	Dinosaurs
208 to 146		Jurassic	
245 to 208		Triassic	
286 to 245	Paleozoic	Permian	Amphibians and Reptiles
360 to 286		Carboniferous	
410 to 360		Devonian	Fishes
440 to 410		Silurian	
505 to 440		Ordovician	Early ocean animals
544 to 505		Cambrian	

The Age of Reptiles

Stegosaurus (model above) was a plant-eating dinosaur. Scientists believe that the plates on its back helped the animal regulate its body temperature.

During the Mesozoic era, dinosaurs and other reptiles ruled the planet. That is why the time between 245 and 65 million years ago is called the Age of Reptiles. Turtles, snakes, and crocodiles also lived on Earth at that time. Many of these creatures lived on land, but some swam in Earth's ancient seas, and others spent most of their time flying through the air.

Scientists working all over the world have identified about 500 different kinds of dinosaurs. Some dinosaurs were as small as a duck. Others were bigger than a house. Some dinosaurs were ferocious predators that tore their prey apart. Others spent their days munching on grass, tree branches, and fruit.

A DINOSAUR NAMED SUE

In 1990, a fossil hunter named Susan Hendrickson found a nearly complete *Tyrannosaurus rex* skeleton on South Dakota's Cheyenne River Sioux Reservation. Two years later, Peter Larson paid a ranch owner on the reservation $5,000 for the dinosaur remains. A few months later, the skeleton—named Sue after its discoverer—was seized by Federal Bureau of Investigation (FBI) agents and National Guard personnel. Because the bones were found on an Indian reservation, Larson should have asked for the government's permission before removing them. In 1995, a court sentenced Larson to two years in jail, and the U.S. government sold Sue's skeleton (above) to the Field Museum in Chicago, Illinois, for more than $8 million.

Fossils of dinosaurs are much less common than fossils of tiny ocean creatures. So why can you see their giant **skeletons** in almost any natural history museum? Because big fossils are more likely to catch our eye and capture our imagination. Dinosaurs are so interesting that scientists have spent a lot of time studying them and searching for their bones.

The Age of Mammals

Millions of years ago, giant ground sloths were common in the American West. They were much larger than the modern sloths that live in Central America.

Scientists believe that the first mammals **evolved** about 230 million years ago. They arose from a group of small reptiles called therapsids. For millions of years, a variety of small mammals shared Earth with dinosaurs and other reptiles. But mammals did not really start to thrive until the dinosaurs died out. That is why the Cenozoic era is called the Age of Mammals.

DID YOU KNOW?

Scientists recently discovered the **skeleton** of a mouse-sized mammal in northeastern China. Using a variety of dating techniques, researchers say that the *Tricodont* fossil is about 145 million years old. That makes it the oldest complete mammal skeleton ever unearthed.

Once the dinosaurs were gone, mammals quickly adapted to fill the roles that the reptiles left behind. Wild dogs and cats became some of Earth's most important predators. Many large, plant-eating mammals also developed.

Today, Earth has about 4,500 kinds of mammals. This large group includes sloths and squirrels, bats and bears, porcupines and porpoises, wolves and weasels, and hyenas and humans. Many other mammals have come and gone.

Other groups of mammals have existed for millions of years, but they have changed a great deal over time. Early horses were smaller than modern horses and had three toes on each foot. Early rhinoceroses had no horns. Mammoths looked similar to modern elephants, but they were larger and had shaggy coats.

WHAT A DISCOVERY!

In 1999, a team of scientists led by Larry Agenbroad of Northern Arizona University excavated an adult male mammoth that was nearly perfectly preserved under layers of Siberian ice. The creature—still surrounded by a giant block of ice—was airlifted by helicopter (above) to a special temperature-controlled underground tunnel in Khatanga, Russia. It is now being studied by scientists from all over the world.

Plant Fossils and Fossil Fuels

The ferns that left behind these fossilized imprints lived during the Carboniferous period of the Paleozoic era. Look at the **geologic time scale** on page 19 to find out about how old the imprints are.

Most plants have soft parts, so fossils of ancient plants are more rare than animal fossils. The majority of plant fossils are imprints. When a plant fell into a lake millions of years ago, its body rotted away, but its shape was left behind in the muddy bottom. When the lake bed hardened to form **sedimentary rock,** the imprint was preserved in stone.

Oil, natural gas, and coal are also the remains of ancient plants. That is why they are called **fossil fuels.** We burn fossil fuels to produce heat and electricity. Fossil fuels are also used to make gasoline, detergents, plastics, nail polish, fertilizer, and other products.

DID YOU KNOW?

Scientists have found fossils of tropical ferns in Antarctica. This suggests that the land that now makes up the chilly Antarctic continent must once have been much closer to the equator.

Oil and natural gas are the remains of tiny ocean plants and animals called **plankton.** When the plankton die, their remains sank to the bottom of the ocean and were buried by layers of mud, sand, and other **sediments.** As time passed, the sediment turned to rock, but the plankton turned into the thick, black liquid we call oil. In the process, the plankton gave off the gas we call natural gas.

Coal is the fossilized remains of swampy forest plants. Over time, the plants were heated and compressed until they became as hard as stone. Scientists also think of coal as a rock. When the plants hardened to form coal, they formed a solid mass of carbon, one of the **minerals** that make up rocks.

A FOSSIL FOREST

When the wood in a tree is replaced with minerals and slowly turns to stone, we say the tree has become **petrified.** Petrified Forest National Park in Arizona features thousands of petrified logs (above). They are the remains of ancient trees like pines that covered the area about 225 million years ago.

Be a Fossil Hunter

Fossils are easier to find than you might think. In fact, you can find them almost anywhere in the world—maybe even in your own backyard. The next time you see a rock, pick it up and look at it closely. There might be a fossil inside.

Most fossils are found in **sedimentary rock.** Very few fossils are found in **igneous rock,** a type that

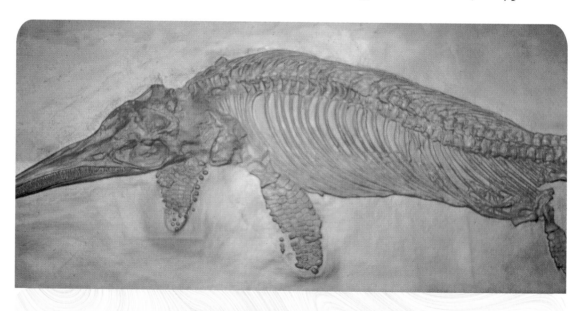

CHILDREN ARE COLLECTORS

As a child, Mary Anning (1799–1847) began collecting shells and fossils near her home in Lyme Regis, England. She didn't keep these treasures, though. She sold them to help support her family. Some people say that the popular tongue twister,

"She sells seashells by the seashore," was written about Mary Anning. Today, the young fossil hunter is best remembered for finding the first fossils of an *Ichthyosaurus*, a large dinosaur that lived in the ocean.

forms when **magma** cools down and hardens. **Metamorphic rock,** formed when other kinds of rock are exposed to tremendous heat or pressure, sometimes contains fossils.

It's fun to hunt for fossils with people who know a lot about them. Call a local nature center or natural history museum and ask whether they organize fossil collecting trips. If you are looking for fossils on your own, you will need to gather a few pieces of equipment and learn some important rules.

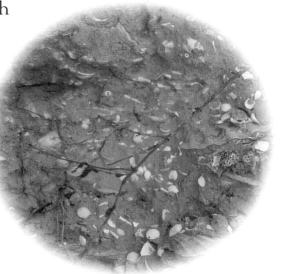

You can see many fossilized shells in this rock. They were found in a riverbed in Virginia.

WHAT YOU NEED

- Hiking boots
- A map and compass
- A pick and a trowel to collect samples
- Safety glasses to keep rock chips out of your eyes
- A small paintbrush to clean dirt and extra rock chips off the samples
- A camera to take photographs of fossils that you are not allowed to collect
- A hand lens to get an up-close look at the fossils
- A notebook for recording when and where you find each fossil
- A field guide to fossils

WHAT YOU NEED TO KNOW

- Never go fossil hunting alone. Go with a group that includes an adult.
- Know how to read a map and use a compass.
- Always get a landowner's permission before walking on private property. If you find fossils, ask the owner if you may remove them.
- Before removing samples from public land, make sure fossil collecting is allowed. The fossils and rock formations at many national parks are protected by law.
- Respect nature. Do not disturb living things, and do not litter.

Studying Fossils

Paleontologists spend many hours carefully examining fossils. These bones were found on a fossil dig in Thailand.

Once you collect some fossils, you will probably want to find out what they are. A good field guide to fossils can help get you started. If you think you have found a really interesting or unusual fossil, you may want to contact a paleontologist—a scientist who studies prehistoric life by examining fossils.

DID YOU KNOW?

More than 2,600 years ago, scientists in ancient Greece understood that fossils were the remains of ancient creatures that no longer lived on Earth. They even suggested that fossils of sea creatures were found on dry land because the land had once been covered by water.

FOSSIL FEUD

Paleontologists are experts at piecing together fossil finds, and they know how to "read" the bones. For example, by looking at fossil teeth, a paleontologist can often tell what an animal ate. If the teeth are large and flat, the animal probably used them to grind tough plants, such as grasses. If the teeth are smaller, sharper, and more pointed, the animal probably used its teeth to tear and chew the flesh of other animals. After studying ancient leg bones or hip bones to see how they fit together, a paleontologist may be able to tell how large an animal was and whether it walked on two legs or four legs.

Saber-tooth cats (below) became extinct about 11,000 years ago. To learn more about them, scientists study modern tigers and cougars.

Paleontologists can also learn about the fossil bones of ancient animals by comparing them to the bones of their living relatives. This process can help scientists understand how the creatures have changed over time.

Glossary

absolute age: age based on tests performed on rock

cast: fossil that forms when minerals harden inside a mold

core: center of Earth. The inner core is solid, and the outer core is liquid.

crust: outer layer of Earth

evolve: to change gradually over time

extinct: died out; gone from Earth forever

fossil fuel: remains of ancient plants that are burned to create heat and electricity

geologic time scale: way scientists divide time so that they can easily understand what Earth was like when various ancient animals lived

igneous rock: kind of rock that forms when magma from Earth's mantle cools and hardens

magma: hot, soft rock that makes up Earth's mantle. When magma spills out onto Earth's surface, it is called lava.

mantle: layer of Earth between the crust and outer core. It is made of soft rock called magma.

metamorphic rock: kind of rock that forms when heat or pressure changes the minerals within igneous rock, sedimentary rock, or another metamorphic rock

mineral: natural solid material with a specific chemical makeup and structure. The "mineral" materials that seep into buried bones are dissolved in water and therefore do not have a true mineral structure. When the water evaporates, the materials re-form their normal mineral structure and harden into true minerals.

mold: imprint of an ancient creature in a rock

petrified: changed into stone; often used to describe the process by which wood becomes a fossil

plankton: tiny creatures that float on top of the water. Plankton is an important source of food for fish and other sea animals.

plate: one of the large slabs of rock that make up Earth's crust

Quaternary period: time we live in, according to the geologic time scale

relative age: age based on the kind of fossils a rock contains

rift: crack in Earth's surface created when two plates move away from each other

sedimentary rock: kind of rock that forms as layers of mud, clay, and tiny rocks build up over time

sediment: mud, clay, and bits of rock picked up by rivers and streams and dumped in the ocean

skeleton: internal bony structure that supports the bodies of many animals

trace fossil: ancient evidence like footprints and trails that tells how, when, or where a creature lived

transform fault: crack that forms on Earth's surface where two plates scrape against each other

To Find Out More

BOOKS

Blobaum, Cindy. *Geology Rocks!: 50 Hands-On Activities to Explore the Earth*. Charlotte, Vt: Williamson, 1999.

Kittinger, Jo S. *Stories in Stone: The World of Animal Fossils*. Danbury, Conn.: Franklin Watts, 1998.

Lessem, Don. *Dinosaurs to Dodos: An Encyclopedia of Extinct Animals*. New York: Scholastic, 1999.

Pellant, Chris. *The Best Book of Fossils, Rocks, and Minerals*. New York: Kingfisher, 2000.

Relf, Patricia. *A Dinosaur Named Sue: The Story of the Colossal Fossil: The World's Most Complete T. Rex*. New York: Scholastic, 2000.

The Simon & Schuster Encyclopedia of Dinosaurs & Prehistoric Creatures: A Visual Who's Who of Prehistoric Life. New York: Simon & Schuster, 1999.

Taylor, Paul D. *Eyewitness: Fossil*. New York: Dorling Kindersley, 2000.

Thompson, Sharon Elaine. *Death Trap: The Story of the La Brea Tar Pits*. Minneapolis: Lerner, 1995.

ORGANIZATIONS

The Field Museum
1400 S. Lake Shore Drive
Chicago, IL 60605
312/922-9410

Natural History Museum
Cromwell Road,
London, UK SW7 5BD
44 (0)20 7942 5011

Index